RAILWAY MOODS

THE MID HANTS RAILWAY

THE WATERCRESS LINE

MATT ALLEN

HALSGROVE

First published in Great Britain in 2007

Copyright © Matt Allen 2007

British Library Cataloguing-in-Publication Data
A CIP record for this title is available from the British Library

ISBN 978 1 84114 604 1

HALSGROVE
Halsgrove House,
Ryelands Farm Industrial Estate,
Bagley Green, Wellington, Somerset TA21 9PZ
Tel: 01823 653777 Fax: 01823 216796
email: sales@halsgrove.com
website: www.halsgrove.com

Printed and bound by D'Auria Industrie Grafiche, Italy

INTRODUCTION

The scenic Mid Hants Railway, 'The Watercress Line' operates heritage steam train services between Alresford and Alton over a distance of approximately 10 miles. This book will take its reader on a journey along the length of the line, depicting a variety of engines and events along the way. Seasons will come and go and come again as we make our way from Alresford towards Alton.

The railway received consent from Parliament in 1861 and in 1865 the Mid Hants Railway (known then as the Alton, Alresford and Winchester Railway Company) was opened. The line originally ran between Winchester and London and soon became a welcomed alternative transport for the local Hampshire Watercress fields. Watercress did not travel well and so the railway enabled distant London markets to be reached, with crops taken daily by horse and cart to Alresford Station.

The Alton, Alresford and Winchester Railway staffed the stations, with the London & South Western Railway providing the rolling stock, locomotives and drivers, eventually becoming a part of the Southern Region of British Railways under nationalisation. The line was closed by British Rail in 1973 as a part of the 'Beeching Plan' and track sections lifted between some of the stations, but an eager group of enthusiasts keen not to see the line disappear forever formed the new 'Mid Hants Railway' and work began to rebuild the line. The line was partially re-opened from Alresford to Ropley in 1977, extending to Medstead in 1983 and in 1985 Alton followed, finally connecting the railway back with the mainline. Unfortunately due to heavy costs the line between Alresford and Winchester with its intermediate station of Itchen Abbas was not re-opened. Extension south will now sadly never be possible due to development on this part of the old line.

Although there were originally five, the line now has four working stations, starting at Alresford, the administrative headquarters, then one at Ropley, where the main locomotive shed and engineering facilities are located, another jointly serving the villages of Medstead and Four Marks and finally terminating at Alton. The section of line between Ropley and Alton is known as 'The Alps', due to long steep gradients of up to 1-in-60, The fifth station, Itchen Abbas on the section from Alresford to Winchester was never re-opened. The whole line is single track, with trains able to pass at Alresford, Ropley and Medstead Stations with an additional passing loop just outside Alton Station.

Today the railway is mostly volunteer run, with regular steam and diesel hauled trains, hosting special events including dining trains, Gala Weekends, Thomas Weekends and Santa Specials. What was the old Lyme Regis station building now hosts a volunteer run café at Alresford Station and the old goods shed has benefited from the Heritage Lottery Fund, enabling a rebuild into a shop with conference facilities upstairs.

The line is now one of the main players of railway preservation thanks in part to its mainline connection at Alton, which means it is often temporary home to 'mainline' steam locomotives whilst they are working specials in the south, being an ideal base to service them. The Mid Hants is also one of Hampshire's biggest tourist attractions; with its steep gradients it is one of the best places in preservation to see steam locomotives really working hard, whilst proving a real challenge for the fireman and driver. The railway is a testament to the effort put in by hundreds of volunteers.   Often unsuspecting travellers driving their cars along the A31 will be surprised to look across and see an impressive steam locomotive reminiscent of years gone by running alongside the adjacent fields!

The Mid Hants is known as not an easy railway to photograph, so it provided a real challenge. Being my 'local' line, I have used my inside knowledge to try and find as many different locations as possible. I hope you enjoy looking at these photos as much as I enjoyed taking them.

This book is dedicated to my father: he would have been so proud.

Matt Allen

MAP OF THE AREA

THE MID HANTS RAILWAY

N

To Basingstoke

ALTON
STATION

Butts Junction

Chawton Woods

MEDSTEAD
& FOUR MARKS
STATION

A31

Summit Of
Mid Hants Railway

A32

To Winchester

ROPLEY STATION
& ENGINE SHED

Wanders Curve

ALRESFORD
STATION

Northside Lane

Drawn by Nick Rowntree

The journey begins. Alresford Station from the road bridge at the north end of the
station provides a grandstand view of the beautifully restored station and headquarters of the railway.
Black 5 number 45231 'Sherwood Forester' is waiting in platform 1 to start its 10 mile journey to Alton.

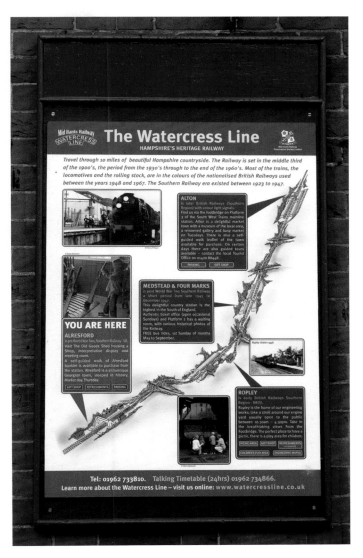

73096 pulls into platform 2 at Alresford from the yard at the far end of the Mid Hants boundary west of the station. This platform is only normally used during galas and busy periods.

Visitors to the Mid Hants Railway get a preview of what the journey has in store and some of the places of interest along the route.

An amazing sight at Alresford. 71000 'Duke of Gloucester' is waiting to leave with the
'Cathedrals Express' mainline steam special to Waterloo (courtesy of the mainline connection at Alton).
The dense fog and smoke combine with the station's gas lights to create a great effect.

A quiet day at Alresford allows for a good view of the station.
The Class 117 DMU waits to leave with a service to Alton.

The old goods shed at Alresford
has been rebuilt and now houses the
railway's shop and conference room.
Inside the the shop is a recreation
of the good sheds office, with
many interesting items on display.

Opposite:
The railway holds a number
of specials events throughout
the year. Here 34016 'Bodmin'
is getting special protection from
the Military Police during
one of the railway's 'War on
the Line' events.

'Waiting for the Right Away'. The driver of 34045 'Ottery St Mary' (actually 34027 'Taw Valley' in disguise) awaits for the right away from Alresford.

12

Alresford Station still has the original gas lamps, which add to the
great atmosphere and original features of the station.

The railway's own dining train, 'The Watercress Belle' awaits its dining passengers on a cold winter's night.

The crew on Standard 5 locomotive 73096 make the final checks before a nightime departure to Alton.

5637 visiting from the East Somerset Railway pulls into platform 1 at Alresford
whilst 92212 waits to shunt onto the front of the train when it is ready.

Southern Railway poster boards complement the authentic look of the station.

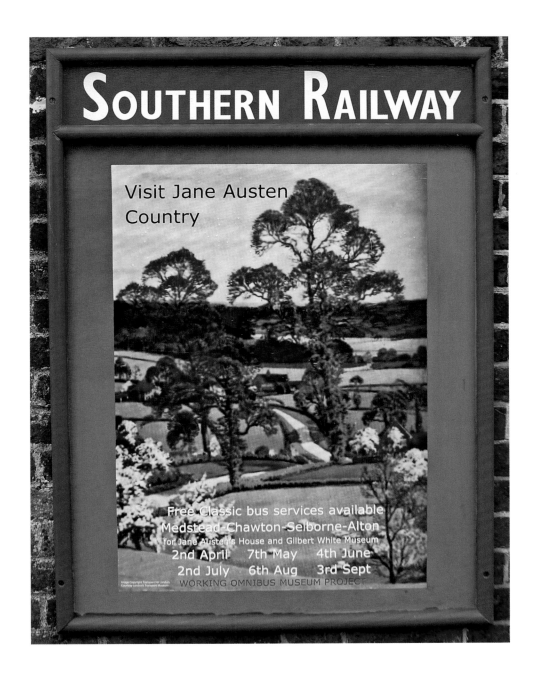

'Little and Large'. 35005 'Canadian Pacific' is waiting to depart as Ivatt 41312
pulls into platform 2 with its demonstration goods train.

Awaiting its next duty, 45231 in the cattle dock at Alresford. In the distance under the bridge you can just see that a down train has the signal. Presumably 45231 will go onto the front of the train when it arrives.

A rather unusual view of a loco passing through the platform,
taken from the inside of a Willis Jeep during a '1940s' event.

Christmas comes to Alresford, with the 'Watercress Belle' ready to serve Christmas dinner steam style.

3440 'City of Truro', a part of the national collection, is unloaded during one of its visits. Coming in by road, unloading is a very difficult task. Road access is via the car park and cattle dock at Alresford.

35005 'Canadian Pacific' one of the very powerful Merchant Navy Class locomotives is framed perfectly by the bridge as it runs around its train. This locomotive has now been purchased by The Mid Hants Preservation Society.

Immediately after leaving Alresford the line goes through Sun Lane cutting (that until very recently) was lined with trees. This rather unusual shot shows Standard 5 73096 working hard as it winds its way through the cutting.

The same viewpoint as the previous picture, minus trees. This now allows for much better views of approaching trains. During busy periods trains can often be signal checked on the approach to the station, as seen in this picture.

Seen from the other end of Sun Lane cutting, the train emerges on the beginning of its journey to Alton. At this point the railway crosses the main B3047 road from Ropley.

Visiting locomotive 4936 'Kinlet Hall' is paired with the Umber and Cream coaches from the 'Watercress Belle', providing an authentic GWR look. Here the train is heading towards Alresford, just before the road bridge.

As the trains leave Alresford they work hard on the climb towards Ropley.
Here 73096 makes a fine exhaust in the cold air.

Not quite the Somerset and Dorset, the classic 'Pines Express'
is recreated authentically with 9Fs 92212 and 92203 in charge.

Diminutive 'Terrier' locomotive No 55 'Stepney' (from Thomas the Tank Engine fame) visiting from its base at the Bluebell Railway. It is seen here making a good head of steam as it makes its approach to Alresford.

The same location as the previous picture, but a train heading towards Ropley. After exiting the cutting and crossing the road, the landscape starts to open out. Engines work hard all the way from Alresford to Ropley.

A timeless picture, there is virtually nothing in it which dates it as 2006.
41312 heads a rake of fantastically restored period freight wagons, giving a glimpse
of freight transportation of the past. 41312 was shedded at various locations on
the Southern during its BR days, so is well at home on the Mid Hants.

Opposite: In recent years the railway has run a rather unusual combination
on Alresford-Ropley shuttles during steam galas. They have run 'push pull'
operations with the DMU trailer car. So whilst the steam loco is applying the
power in both directions, there is no need to run the steam loco round.

Beattie Well Tank no 30585 was a visitor to the railway and is seen here
on a demonstration freight train, en route from Alresford to Ropely.

Occasionally the railway is the destination for railtours (thanks to its mainline connect at Alton).
Here Hastings Unit 1001 is on the 'Mid Hants Venturer' railtour from Ashford in Kent to Alresford.
These DEMUs are very similar to the 205 class that would have run over Mid Hants metals in BR days.

Spring flowers add extra interest in this picture of the Standard 5 continuing on the climb to Ropley.

Visitor 71000 'Duke of Gloucester' is seen at Bishops Sutton, edging closer towards Ropley.
The 'Phoenix Rising' headboard reflects the condition this one-off locomotive was in
when rescued from Barry Scrapyard. It truly has risen from the flames.

The same location as the previous picture, but from the lineside. 35005 complete with 'The Royal Wessex' headboard comes under the road bridge where the previous picture was taken.

Another visitor from the Bluebell Railway seen here is B4 'Normandy'. This locomotive has a local history having once been the station pilot at Winchester. The Hampshire countryside provides a great backdrop to this short freight train.

Whilst up trains are working hard, again at Northside Lane Bridge we see 'Canadian Pacific' 35005, coasting in the opposite direction towards Alresford.

Silhouetted perfectly, Jinty 47493 is returning to Ropley 'light engine' after a hard day's work.

Opposite: During one of the 'Duke of Gloucester's' visits, the railway held a Pacific weekend
(Pacific – referring to the locomotive's wheel arrangement); 34016 and 35005 were also both in action.
The Duke is seen here at Ropley Distant Signal, just east of Northside Lane.

Viewed from high up on the fields opposite, a train makes the climb towards
Ropley from Alresford. Northside Road Bridge is just visible.

A timeless sight in the Hampshire countryside. Terrier 662 in London and Brighton South Coast Railway livery, seen at Northside Lane on a demonstration freight train.

'Top and Tail'. 47493 is approaching Ropley with a shuttle from Alresford.
Hardly visible apart from its smoke, 'Douglas' (a converted J94) is attached to
the rear of the train, hence the 'Top and Tail'.

The part of the line around Northside Lane is a great place to catch sunsets, allowing for some wonderful shots.

The Pullman coach is a new addition to the Mid-Hants fleet. Car 851 one of the 1960's
Metro Cammell Pullman coaches will be used on the luxury dining trains.

With the mid day sun high above illuminating the smoke,
USA tank number 30075 pilots D6593 seen here approaching Ropley.

Early and late in the day can provide some of the best light.
Here the low winter sun and huge smoke trail make a great spectacle.

The original signals at Ropley provide
great additional interest, especially
when combined with winter sunsets.

After passing Ropley Distant Signal the
train rounds the curve and leaves the single
track on the approach to Ropley Station.
The station footbridge provides an ideal
point to watch the trains arriving.

The view of Ropley Station from the Alresford end. Ropley is a great place to break your journey as it is home to the railway's engine shed and has a large picnic area.

Ropley Station, viewed from the Alton end. 71000 adds extra interest sitting in the platform.

The crossing at the end of Ropley platform says
'Shut this gate' for obvious reasons!

Quite an unusual sight, an engineer's train featuring the steam crane, in the platform at Ropley. The signal box on the left was originally from Netley and is equipped with a 38 lever frame from Barnstaple Junction.

Destination Alresford and not Penzance as the roller blind displays!
The Class 121 'Bubble Car' leaves Ropley on a winter service.

The booking hall at Ropley
provides an unusual viewpoint
to see 34016 'Bodmin'.

73096 waits for 'Bodmin' to pull into platform 1 at Ropley before it will receive the signal token and permission to depart. Note the ongoing work to extend that platform to accommodate longer trains.

Another great sunset at Ropley.

The driver of 30585 (on a visit from the Buckingham Railway Centre) awaits permission to depart Ropley.

Early morning light, combines with smoke and steam to great effect. Terrier 662 visited the line from the Bressingham Steam Centre during a Branchline Gala. These events give the chance to use some smaller engines on shorter trains.

59

Authentic signs add to the feel of the railway. Here an original
LSWR sign guards the crossing at Ropley, whilst 'Bodmin' departs.

Opposite: The double track in the station section at Ropley allows for
trains to pass each other. During busy periods this is one of the best places
to watch trains come and go as there is always something going on.

An historic wheel is mounted at the east end of Ropley Station. The wheel made at Woolwich Arsenal in the 1860s was never used on a locomotive when built due to an imperfection but found another use on a gun carriage instead. It eventually found its way to the Royal Aircraft Establishment at Farnborough from where it was rescued.

9F 92212 sits in the platform whilst waiting for the signal to depart light engine to Alton. With the engine shed at Ropley, locos run light engine in the mornings to both Alton and Alresford to begin the day's services.

Viewed from the north end of Ropley Station, the diesel 350hp
shunter is in use on an engineer's train.

Ropley Motive Power Depot adopts an LMS guise with locos 45231 and 47493. The strange looking
piece of rolling stock on the far right used to be a test bed for DEMU engines at Eastleigh,
but has been brought to the MHR to utilise its chassis, hence its stripped down state.

A rather busy Ropley MPD viewed from the picnic site.
Locomotives 73096, 35005, 34016, 92212, 45231 and a selection of diesels are all present.

Depots and yards are always wet, oily and dirty places, but also allow for some unusual pictures. 71000 creates a great reflection in a puddle.

A brief motive power shortage led to a visit from Collett number 3205 a
Great Western invader! Its visit was so short I never actually saw the loco in action.

Most parts of the yard at Ropley are publicly accessible allowing you to get up close and personal with the locomotives. Nevertheless, some areas including the engine shed itself are out of bounds for the public.

Gala Days with their intensive action make Ropley a hive of activity. With Ropley being in the middle of the line, engines need to be despatched to Alton and Alresford in good time. The view from Bighton Road Bridge is a good place to see these movements.

Electro Diesel number 73107 'Spitfire' is visiting the railway having been used to return a rake of mainline coaches to the MHR after use on a railtour. The 73 operated and owned by Fragonset was repainted especially for the railtour organised by the Shepherd Neame Brewery.

Ropley MPD is the main engineering base of the railway. Not only are running repairs carried out, but long-term restorations are done here also. A4 'Bittern' is seen here part way through a complete rebuild. Steam locomotives need to be completely rebuilt every ten years at great cost.

Opposite:
West Country class 'Bodmin' takes a rest in the yard at Ropley. The locomotive would have run over Mid Hants' metals in steam days and were the backbone of express passenger trains on the Southern.

Under the lights, 9F 92212 almost looks as if it were on stage, on a cold December evening at Ropley.

Due to its location, the railway is often used as a base for mainline steam locomotives in between duties. Here 34027 'Taw Valley' (seen here running as 34045 'Ottery St Mary') is a brief visitor whilst on 'Cathedrals Express' duties in the south of England.

Another visitor to the railway during a stint of mainline specials in the south is A4 locomotive 60009 'Union of South Africa'. Seen here at Ropley with another Pacific, this time resident West Country Pacific 'Bodmin'.

45231, a Class 5 and 71000, classified an 8P, sit in the yard outside Ropley MPD.

The 9F looks ready to depart, but is just missing its crew! The fireman has his shovel positioned in place and the signalman has hung the signal token over the door.

The Mid Hants doesn't have a huge diesel fleet, this Class 33 D6593 being the railway's resident diesel work horse, fitting in perfectly with its 1960's 'as new' livery. These locomotives would have run over the Mid Hants under BR ownership.

A new addition to the engineering facilities at Ropley is the wheel drop, purpose built to carry out advanced repairs to wheel sets. 4160, a visitor to the line, experienced problems with its wheel sets, so it was lucky the wheel drop had been commissioned!

Snow in Hampshire is rare these days. 45231 is also mainline certified and looks like it has returned from mainline duties as it is still coupled to its support coach.

Just north of the MPD and yard are the storage sidings for locomotives awaiting long-term restoration.
Un-rebuilt Bulleid Pacific 34105 'Swanage' once a regular performer in preservation makes a rather sad sight.
The line climbing away towards Medstead can just be seen in the far right.

The 9F is approaching Ropley from Medstead.
Quite often the approaching trains are checked at the signal.

Leaving Ropley heading towards Medstead and Alton 'The Alps' begin. This formidable 1-60 climb all the way to Medstead is know locally as 'The Alps' for obvious reasons. This is one of the most testing climbs on any preserved railway.

A great view of the climb, this picture really shows how steep and straight the line is. The sight and sounds of 73096 climbing up the bank is something I shall never forget. In the far distance you can just make out the storage sidings north of Ropley yard.

The railway has held Diesel Galas in the past, which attracted visiting
locomotives. Here English Electric Class 37, number 37190 makes
an impressive sight attacking the climb out of Ropley.

In full GWR livery Prairie number 5542 is starting the climb out of Ropley. These locomotives would have been commonplace on GWR branchlines, but would have been a rarity in rural Hampshire.

As the climb out of Ropley continues, the embankment gradually gets higher and more impressive. Here 30075 is approaching Stable Lane Bridge.

32473 originally built in 1898 was one of the 0-6-2 Stroudley tank locomotives. The locomotive has visited from its base at the Bluebell on a number of occasions. It is seen here heading down the bank towards Ropley.

With my head in the cabbages! A different viewpoint that somehow makes the embankment look smaller than it really is.

Opposite: The 'Mid Day Scot' in the heart of Hampshire. 71000 'Duke of Gloucester' regularly uses the railway as a base between mainline duties in the south (far from its home at the East Lancs Railway at Bury).

71000 emerges from Wanders Curve on a dreary summer's day, framed perfectly by the trees.

Electro Diesel number 73107 'Spitfire' was a visitor to the railway, having been used to return a rake of coaches after use on a mainline railtour. To get the loco from Ropley back to the mainline at Alton, it was attached to the back of a service train (in this case the Class 117 DMU), hence this unusual combination.

Merchant Navy Class locomotive 'Canadian Pacific' number 35005 (known affectionately as 'Can Pac') is seen crossing Stable Lane Bridge. Despite running down the bank from Medstead to Ropley it seems to be working quite hard.

71000 'The Duke' makes great smoke effects, enjoyed by the enthusiasts at the windows of the coaches. This locomotive was allocated to Crewe Depot during its steam days so is unlikely to have worked over the Mid Hants prior to its closure.

Just south of Wanders Curve 2MT 41312 rolls down The Alps towards Ropley. These engines were a common sight on the Southern during the end of steam, being used on a number of branchlines and also as station pilots at Waterloo.

Two of Bulleid's finest, 34016 'Bodmin' and the more powerful 35005 'Canadian Pacific' look rather out of proportion on a four-coach train, coasting towards Ropley from Medstead. Galas often allow for 'Double Headed' operations to add more interest.

You can't beat a clear winter's day for dramatic pictures.

Peak 45112 adds some colour to this very green scene! This engine was visiting the railway for a gala,
although the railway does have its own resident Peak 45132, which is currently out for long-term repairs.

'A pair of fives'. Standard 5MT 73096 pilots Black 5 45231 just north of Wanders Curve.
The section from Wanders Curve towards Medstead rises high on the embankment. This is clearly
visible from the main A31: what must the car drivers think when they catch sight of a view like this!

73096 was withdrawn from BR service in November 1967.
I bet no one would have imagined a sight like this 38 years later.

34016 approaching Wanders Crossing as it rolls downhill towards Ropley.
Coasting down the 1 in 60 is normally harder on the brakes than anything else.

'Gala Day'. This unusual combination of 45231 'Sherwood Forester', 3440 'City of Truro' and 34016 'Bodmin' work light engine from Ropley to Alton in readiness for the day's trains. Surely the first time such a combination has been seen.

Early spring can produce some stunning light. Here 35005 'Canadian Pacific' is illuminated to great affect. The Alps making the engine work very hard.

Caught at speed in this 'panned' shot, 35005 is attacking The Alps.

Opposite: 'Canadian Pacific' is seen entering Soldridge Cutting further along the bank.

The last rays of sun from a winter's day create great light as 9F 92212 heads down the bank towards Ropley.

This is the last part of the line visible from the road. The embankment turns into a cutting flanked by houses on the final climb to Medstead and Four Marks Station. E4 locomotive number 32473 is seen here with a local service from Ropley to Alton.

9F 92212 was built at Swindon in September 1959 and only lasted in BR service until January 1968, an incredibly short working life. Luckily it was rescued from Woodhams Scrapyard and now gives us sights like this.

A final shot of the embankment adjacent to the A31. Smoke is sent spiralling into the air by 71000. This locomotive was deemed a failure during its very brief BR service; however, modifications in preservation to rectify a number of design faults have turned it into a sterling performer.

One of O.S.V. Bulleid-designed West Country Class locomotive 'Bodmin' pulls an Alresford-bound train into the platform at a very grey Medstead.

Opposite: Porters await the arrival of a train from Ropley. The original signal box at Medstead (officially known as Medstead and Four Marks) was demolished. The one you can see in the picture was originally from Wilton South. The station has been restored to Southern Railway 1930's standard.

A GWR classic in the heart of Southern Territory!

Opposite: Gala Days at the railway provide an opportunity to run an intensive train service and hire in visiting locomotives. Here visiting loco 4936 'Kinlet Hall' passes resident 73096 at Medstead Station.

The only passing points on the line are Alresford, Ropley and Medstead Stations and the loop just outside Alton Station. 34016 is waiting for Ivatt 41312 to pull into the station before it can receive the token from the signalman and depart for Alton.

WARNING
STOP LOOK & LISTEN
BEFORE CROSSING THE LINE

L. & S.W.R.
PASSENGERS
MUST CROSS LINE
BY BRIDGE

A demonstration freight waiting to leave
Medstead. The mix of bauxite and grey
wagons matching BR-era-liveried 41312.

Catching up with the day's news at
Medstead and Four Marks circa 1939...
well almost.

3440 'City of Truro' heads into Medstead from Alton. Just beyond the end of the train is the summit of the railway at 650 feet above sea level. After having climbed from Alton to Medstead 3440 will be glad of the rest as it rolls down the bank to Ropley.

A truly nostalgic '60's scene. The Triumph 3TA motorcycle built in 1964
sitting on the platform and the 9F built in 1959 pulling into Medstead.

Medstead is also the home of the railway's Permanent Way and Infrastructure Departments.
On a random visit to the station I was quite surprised by the motive power on display!

East of Medstead is a very steep and deep cutting called Shrave Cutting. 45231 is seen here entering the cutting from Alton in the middle of a brief snow shower.

There are some good vantage points around Brick Kiln Farm to watch trains exiting
Chawton Woods. The section from the summit just north of Medstead to Alton is downhill,
although of course trains from Alton (as seen here) will be climbing hard.

The rather unusual sight of steam and diesel top and tail. During one of the railway special events USA Tank 30075 struggled with the steep gradients so D6593 was called in to assist.

Chawton Woods adorn the steep climb parallel with the A31 from Alton to Medstead. Here 3440 is viewed from the top of the adjacent hills. A bit of a trek to the top, but the views are well worth it.

35005 'Canadian Pacific' is pictured here making its comeback after lengthy repairs.
A Sunday lunchtime 'Watercress Belle' it is seen returning its diners to Alresford.

With its steep banks the Mid Hants is a true test for any engine. There are very few flat parts of the line, so the engines are working hard or hard on the brakes. Visiting 9F 92203 'Black Prince' and resident Bulleid Pacific 34016 'Bodmin' make a colourful combination during a summer gala.

Opposite: Scotrail in rural Hampshire! During one of the railway's Diesel Galas a pair of English Electric class 37s make a stunning sight. The lead locomotive is in the classic Scotrail Large Logo livery complete with Scottie dog (a sign the loco was allocated to Eastfield Shed) on the side.

Western Ranger D1013 in bright sunshine climbs out of Chawton Woods.

71000 'Duke of Gloucester' is heading for Medstead with a 'Santa Special' from Alton. The locomotive was at the railway for repairs following problems on a mainline run; the 'Santa Special' is effectively its test run.

The section of line through Chawton Woods can be quite difficult to photograph due to the lineside vegetation and tall trees. However, during the winter when there are no leaves on the trees there are brief glimpses of the train. 34016 creates great plumes on the climb towards Medstead.

On 9 May 1904 'City of Truro' became the first locomotive to reach 100 mph. Despite its three-coach loading here the GWR veteran won't be going any faster than 25mph, the speed limit for the Mid Hants.

92212 is due for overhaul soon, although this picture gives no indication of that at all.

This picture sums up the Mid Hants perfectly, with trains working hard up the steep gradients. Here 34016 is climbing through Chawton Woods heading from Alton towards Medstead.

The 2-10-0 wheel arrangement of the 9Fs was designed for hauling heavy freight trains, so passenger trains at the Mid Hants pose no problem for such powerful engines.

Opposite: Sometimes rain showers can be a photographer's friend! The train was running a bit late and I didn't think the rainbow would last, but luckily it did! 5542 is framed by the rainbow contrasting with a very angry sky.

A fine view from the hill overlooking Chawton Woods. 92212 looks splendid with its train of BR Mark 1 coaches.

Moving nearer towards Alton, this is the site of Butts Junction. This is were there was a spur that went to Basingstoke. The building on the left is what's left of Butts Junction signal box. At this point the main road from Basingstoke also passes under the railway.

Exactly the same location as the previous picture but from the roadside.

During times of heavy leaf fall or frosty conditions, occasionally a diesel is attached to the back of train as insurance over the steep gradients. This is quite common on the first train of the day when the rail conditions are unknown. Here D6593 is attached to the back of a train. The gradient towards Medstead from Alton is also fairly apparent.

A view of Alton signal box from the other side, as 73096 is just approaching Alton Station.

Opposite: A train departing Alton and the start of the passing loop just outside the signal box is just visible. The platform at Alton is only a single track, with a
run round loop to enable the locomotive to run from one end of the train to another.

Alton is the end of the 10-mile
journey from Alresford, and is
where the railway connects with the
national network. From Alton
you can get direct trains to
Waterloo via Woking.

'Where old and new collide'.
73096 pulls into the Mid Hants
platform, whilst a new Desiro
electric unit waits in the South
West Trains platform with a
train for Waterloo.

The Mid Hants retains a connection to the mainline, so specials are able to run through from Network Rail territory onto the Mid Hants. Here is a rather unusual shot of the gate open as a pair of Class 50 diesels leave the Mid Hants with a 'Pathfinder Tours' special returning to Sheffield.

A bird's-eye view of Alton Station taken from the footbridge. The platform to the far left is the Mid Hants platform and the other two belong to South West Trains. You can also see the gate which marks the spot where the Mid Hants joins the mainline. This is controlled and opened by Network Rail as required, as seen in the previous picture.

The fireman of 73096 awaits the
signal to depart, the fire from the
firebox can be seen reflecting
on the cab.

Alton Station still maintains some of its original charm and offers a choice of trains.
A modern Desiro electric unit to London, or steam train to Alresford…
I know which I'd choose!